Letters Inscribed in Snow

LETTERS INSCRIBED IN SNOW

Laynie Browne

**TINDERBOX
EDITIONS**

Tinderbox Editions
Molly Sutton Kiefer, Publisher and Editor
Red Wing, Minnesota
tinderboxeditions@gmail.com
www.tinderboxeditions.org

Cover design by Nikkita Cohoon
Cover art by Erica Baum. Head Band ("Naked Eye"), 2012, archival-pigment print, 15 1/2 × 17 7/10 inches, by courtesy of the artist and Bureau, New York City.
Interior design by Nikkita Cohoon

come love, enter

"Love is the same and does not keep that name
I keep that name and I am not the same"

—Bernadette Mayer from *Midwinter Day*

"The book, traveling backward, holds a smaller book, which it
is reading.
a book is however, an acceleration, or causes one."

—Rachel Blau DuPlessis from *Surge: Drafts 96-114*

"And all of the many sheets of paper that I inscribed at the top with
my name and that address were never used for writing letters but
to write this novel, which, at least to begin with definitely had the
form of a series of letters, though I never intended that they be put
in envelopes and mailed like letters: you might look at the whole
thing as a result of the habit I had when I wrote letters as often and
painstakingly as you wash your hands. Several times a day."

—Inger Christensen from *Azorno*

"Some looked like huge loathsome porcupines, others like whole
knots of snakes that stuck forth their heads, and others like fat little
bears with bristly hair— all shining white, all living snowflakes."

—Hans Christian Anderso from *The Snow Queen*

Contents

Letters Inscribed in Snow

I. An Opening

We are standing in a gallery looking at the floor. Embedded, sunken, is a four-foot by four-foot square slab of ice, opaque white. Around the slab is a rope, officially cordoning off the area. A plaque on the wall upon entering the small room reads, "A Book Inscribed in Snow." The ice is blank, bare. The artist did not show up for the opening. We find out later that the artist used a pseudonym. An agent installed the piece and departed. Failed to answer questions. The artist clearly intended an unwritten and therefore open book. Surely the real author or the artist would come forward. But what does that mean—the real author—of snow, of the found, of letters, of invisibility? Bodies standing on frozen ground in winter. Trying to divine what is written beneath. Upon which inscription do you stand?

dear—

I wish I were writing my new novel, but I have not yet begun.
Though I've taken notes many times, beginning with a series
of dream letters, inscribed in snow. My thoughts are still too
unformed. When the right fictional story (which I plan to steal)
falls in front of me, I will begin.

And one of the central questions will be: Is the writer writing to /
obsessed with someone living or dead? Imagined or real? Or is the
one writing the letters the construct?

And another will be, what is a letter? Or maybe the book is made
up entirely of journal entries, found on the pavement. Or about
to be published by one who has died or vanished, or fictional
accounts of dying, or dying as an impetus for correspondence.

Yes, I love you.

How will the book begin?

Sitting in a café, I put down the chain of letters I had been reading. They were published under your name but I was doubtful. You have many names and this was one encoded, an anagram of your enclave, but also a symbol used by a collective of writers who write nothing. You say, in a multi-authored statement, that writing now is lifting, recontextualizing the abundant texts already existent. You say that writing is amplifying, that writers perform as a modern circulatory system. A nervous system, testing impulses up and down avenues, axes, venues of ether, and performative bodies.

I was supposed to meet you at the café. I put the chain of dream letters back into my bag and tried to concentrate, my head bent over my laptop and piles of papers. I kept looking up at the plate glass window, beaded with rain, each time the door opened. In came many faces covered with water, and coats buttoned tight. But each time I looked up, it was not you who entered, and after a while I lost track of how long I had been waiting. What an endless chain of persons who are not you. Suddenly when you did appear, I closed my eyes for a moment because I disbelieved what I saw. How could it be you? You were smiling and suddenly there was no distance between us but even though I recognized you, what I recognized was not your person. Is that possible? The moment furled and unfurled. I was standing to greet you. Distance closed around us, the enormity of having never before met in person, unless once years ago. Or was that imagined? I'm not sure because in our correspondence once, when I was brave enough to mention it, you behaved as if I had said nothing.

Later you sent me a message I did not understand. I had wished for a spectacular meeting and instead I wondered if I had been speaking to a blank composition book. The message relayed an unsolved mathematical problem, which you noted as the most notorious problem in theoretical computer science. You summarized the problem like this: P=NP? You mentioned that the problem would be difficult to paraphrase, but practical applications included cryptography. If the solution to a problem can be verified in polynomial time, can it be inscribed? In order to find a solution, one must first locate a book of exponential time. But your words disorient my meaning. What is your meaning? You try to overcome the difficulty of unsolved problems by breaking down the separation between the body of the known and the unknown. You tell me that this is how you define art. You ask me to join you in this project of decoding the absent book of dream letters. I agree, though I do not entirely grasp your motives.

We are standing in a gallery looking at the floor. Embedded, sunken into our memory, a four-foot by four-foot square slab of ice, opaque white. The space is still surrounded in rope. A plaque on the wall reads: "Here was once installed *Letters Inscribed in Snow.*" The ice has been removed. You did not show up for the meeting of the enclave. I was surprised that when I looked down into the sunken space, I saw a pile of papers. Who had left them? Whoever it was clearly intended for us to find them. Was it the artist or someone else? But what does that mean—the real author—of letters, of intent, of anonymity? Bodies trying to determine which hand should reach in and retrieve the letters. Above whose inscription do we stand? The letters were white, opaque, eroding. Around one notion of already published texts, now another set of letters might continually enlarge us. As we stood examining the bundle, once absent, now actual.

dear—

That version of me on paper is too mild, flat, sentimental. I don't recognize myself. Now I've stopped writing titles entirely. It is so tiresome not knowing how to begin. What to call oneself.

Your words borrow me. I wish I could be calm. But your words disorient my meaning. I am never at home except in receiving your letters. Maybe that is too extreme a statement. Instead I should say—since I cannot draw you. Since I cannot come closer than ice.

A letter inscribed in snow is prone to either melting into water and disappearing or freezing and cracking beneath one's step. How can I know if I read you?

I found this dream letter inscribed to me in snow.

How much do you know about the ground on which you stand? White, opaque, eroding. Around one notion of a planetary system is another which continually enlarges our sight. As we stood examining the absent letter in snow you began to speak about a recent discovery. Scientists have spotted a new dwarf planet at the edge of our solar system. Pink ice far beyond Pluto. Astronomers used to believe there was nothing in this area. Until recently, the only object detected in that part of our solar system was a dwarf planet called Sedna, named after an Inuit goddess said to live in the frigid Arctic Ocean. When we left the gallery you continued to talk about sight, about planetary systems, about ice as preserver.

We were still looking down to the ground covered in ice. I was curious about the artist. Shall we call her Sedna, you asked? Smiling, you reached for my hand, but when I searched your face, your expression was, a moment later, blank, bare. I wanted to discuss the identity of the missing artist, or the unwritten story. But you continued to tell me that the difficulty in sighting more objects in this region is that such distant planets don't emit their own light. Light from the sun has to travel billions of miles out, reflect off the object, then travel billions of miles back. Along the way some light is lost.

Imagine, you say to me, that we are standing on this newly discovered planet. So new it has not been given a name. It's known as 1012VP113. If we were standing on this ball of ice it would be minus four hundred degrees Fahrenheit. And dark. Our sun would appear only as an ordinary, distant star.

dear—

What I really want to know (that is, what the character in the book will want to know) why am I writing this fiction when I have a perfectly reliable life? I have a perfectly remarkable problem I cannot solve. A dream is transparent only to me and is the safety of that which cannot be taken. I must reverse. It takes a very potent illusion. Why now, am I addicted to abandonment, hidden to my motives? Where is the one who walks into the light, across a frozen letter, wearing only a smile? And that is enough.

dear—

I will go and visit my fences now, the ones that keep me sane, such as the borders of any body or book, the borders of time and light, borders of what is said and unsaid. I like to mess with these borders, to know they are in place to some extent but then to stroke or subvert them.

Everything is a lie. There is no separation of bodies. We are less than a myth of ourselves. And aging is another lie, what we look like, how we rely upon ideas of ourselves. Humility comes later, when we work harder to keep ourselves intact.

I try to forget pain through pleasure, through trying to break down any separation between my body and the body of my lover, who is willing and brilliant, but does not entirely grasp my motives.

When I ask about the chain of dream letters inscribed in snow you pause from your calculations and look up at me. We are sitting in your studio, on cement floors. All around us are printouts of statistics, long vertical equations. Letters I have sent to you. Poems created by formulas. Exquisite corpse drawings. The bed is unmade, covered in star maps and texts by Kepler, Einstein, Archimedes, and Euclid. You look at me as if some deterministic polynomial-time has been thrust between us. You look at me as if to solve for "x" were comparable to violence. You must have known that I was not asking if you or your enclave had written or found the letters. You looked me as if to say, how could I possibly ask to whom the letters were written? In this moment of non-speech between us I saw clearly that I was being accused, but of what I was being accused I had no idea. A book of silence instantaneously arose. Did your gaze communicate animosity that I did not know what I should certainly know? Either I was the "you" to whom the letters were addressed, or the mentioned lover, or it was someone else in our small circle. Probably, it was someone who had been standing around that night at the gallery, looking at the blank slab of snow. This was in fact the real reason why the publication of the letters, their circulation, had gained so much attention. The letters were an endless source of speculation.

There we were at all hours of the night, groping on hands on knees, with pencils and pages, tall glasses of tea. We were Turing machines, binary representations, working on this question of completeness, nakedness, on conditions, positions which might satisfy a question. We had become the question in episodic wanderings. We knew nothing about integers or time, but we became an architecture about the mathematics of nondeterministic futures.

dear —

I found this inscription in blood letters, drowned ice

In darkness I bound the blood letters to air

Which aspects of the frozen are real?

But what is it you want to solve, I asked? You answered that you wanted to determine the secret identity of the artist. Even though you were grateful for the hiddenness which had become an opening. An opening which many, including your enclave, rushed in to fill.

Roughly speaking, P is a set of relatively easy problems, and NP is a set of extremely difficult problems, so P = NP would imply that the apparently hard problems actually have relatively easy solutions. But the details are more complicated. The details, you explained are actually persons.

NP (which stands for nondeterministic polynomial time) is the set of problems whose solutions can be verified in polynomial time. But as far as anyone can tell, many of those problems take exponential time to solve. Perhaps the most famous problem in NP, for example, is finding prime factors of a large number. Verifying a solution requires multiplication, but solving the problem seems to require systematically trying out lots of candidates.

And now you look at me again as if we had become an elusive equation, and ask, how will we lure the candidates?

You have narrowed things down, nonsensically, and together we devise a series of questions, of tests, of performances, which first we will try out upon strangers. We begin by planting additional letters in places likely to be noted by our culprits.

dear—

If I told you how often, repeating the same actions, our bodies ache and transfer belief you might note some incongruity between our thinking and irrevocable forms. I speak your hidden name silently and often fear that I might speak it aloud. Instead we make inaudible sounds. Breath in the throat. Or moan loudly. And pray. That you may wake the reliable edges of my body, shatter, erase them permanently. That when it will be time to rise we will still have discernable forms. That we may smile and rise and walk into the world as if we were whole, as if we were complete, as if we really did inhabit, intuit individual forms.

dear—

You sat in my seat representing me. A sheet of ice.

Being empathetically with you is a language. I read the same words as a way of being with you. In all that you say or do is a sound, a synonym.

dear—

You speak as if you wore the Kuiper belt.

As if the region beyond the planets of our solar system, beyond the orbit of Neptune belonged to you. As if you consisted of many small bodies, remnants. As though you were constructed of frozen volatiles, ice.

Sedna has been enlisted in our mathematical derivations. Of course that is not her real name. I don't know when this happened, when all names became fictions, when such fictions or persons began to accompany me. We are walking to the gallery. The bundle of letters is in my bag. I haven't told Sedna that they were entrusted to me. I'm not sure exactly why. I also haven't asked her anything about her interactions with you. I try not to think about her sitting on your cement floors, representing me.

That version of me, become her, is too mild, flat, sentimental. I don't recognize myself. Now I've stopped trying to solve entirely, the problem you speak about as virtual love. A collection of names through which you exist.

Sedna's words borrow me. I wish I could be calm. But her words disorient my meaning. She claims to be never inside herself. Maybe that is too extreme a statement. Instead I should say—

I am melting into water and disappearing, or freezing and cracking beneath your step. How can I know if I read you?

She puts down the pages and looks at me with an agitation I cannot describe. She asks, when did this happen? I say nothing, but offer her another page of the dream letters. She reads the first line aloud:

You speak as if you wore the Kuiper belt.

She puts the page down again, and asks, do you know Halimede well? I suppose it doesn't matter which one of your fictional names she chooses, but that one makes me laugh. She interrupts, unsatisfied by my answer—insists that I tell her.

Sedna, I say, I too am curious about the artist.

Stop calling me that. Could we speak to the author?

But the author has not yet been discovered, has not been given a name.

Later, I am in the café, thinking about walking with Sedna, about the letters in my bag, my potential to crack or melt, your elusiveness. I had been sitting there for what seemed hours and you did not show up. Then he appeared, a man named Metis. For a long time I noticed him watching me as I wrote. Eventually as we were both packing up for the late freeze outdoors, I told him that I had left my cell phone, wallet, cash, ID, credit cards and key to my apartment at your flat, accidentally. That you were probably with Sedna. He asked if I were hungry and invited me for dinner. And there I was moved to confess that I had come to town to try to salvage our relationship, but that I had decided today to abandon any hope. That I was in town also to give a performance. Soon enough, he was passing twenty dollar bills across the table, along with his address. I thanked him profusely and assured him that the loan would be repaid. He looked at me with a warmth not entirely concealing his doubt.

dear—

Who is the one walking, speaking, looking exhausted? The one who prefers to stay hidden.

I tried to interpret each time the light fell. Each time under the open sky. In every register I subscribed to the same danger. Of you and I and the disappearance of the world.

And yet we never disappeared entirely. Invisibility was a myth that kept us. And suspends us still.

dear—

All day long, sitting in various performances. We pretend this isn't
happening. We act as if—.

You interrupt my silence, repeating my name.

This is the path that leads to being barely able to breathe. But now
I am awake. I know where it leads.

dear—

I meet Metis early the next morning and return his loan. He says he is glad he could help. I thank him for attending my performance. He looks at me blankly. And then I confess that it was our entire conversation of yesterday which was the performance. To perform this question, *what it may be like to depend upon the kindness of strangers.*

Metis listens attentively, and then asks me, in what sense, if any, am I still acting?

He enters into my line of light, equipped with only this question. And that is enough. Then he asks me my name.

Sedna, I tell him.

dear—

I speak to you with my fingers wishing to locate solidity, to stop appropriating a danger I associate with unreality.

But then I realize, although I am safe in my imaginative wanderings, that the expression on my face might reveal something. Am I transparent? I might be observed. I feared that anyone could read my thoughts. How could I be so careless with my face?

II. Letters Inscribed in Snow

Dear Kai,

Snowflakes grew bigger and bigger. At last they looked like big white hens.

Games glass in your eye. I almost saw, held up in the rim of. Not quite pressed to lips. As if you were ducking. Dunking in frustration night after noon after riding all day. I don't know what to call you from such a distance.

How could you still populate letters with lucid thoughts? One half of our conversation has ended. Become fluent. Even after I write these words, and then delete them, they reappear. Do you recognize your name, from among your many names? Undertake— to apprentice your name?

Love,
Gerda

You came up behind me and touched my shoulders as I was reading and I put the pages down. I put down the damp eyes of the non-sleeper, and the birded darkness, and the river of unsent messages. Yet as you questioned me, as to whether I would be able to undertake the performance of the tale, I thought that though your pages rested on the table between us, and though I was taken now nowhere else but had been nimbly threaded inside your eyes, I would be unable.

Why, you ask?

I won't be performing. But inhabiting. It's already happened.

shoes—river
flowers—earth

dear—

Go alone threading—echo

You sleep at the feet of distant planets. Newly discovered cold, orbiting.

Written sky or bird. A bird isn't written. Isn't immune to darkness, isn't taken to bed.

Your eyes close damply.

Is there another name for you as in darkness when you cannot be seen?

I don't believe you aren't actual just because I can't hear your language-object song, just because rest is not to be found upon the back of a reindeer, just because I tried to inhabit a river, to sleep on an absent sleigh.

Dear Kai,

Are you still freezing?

Once you were close enough to touch, walked out amid flower boxes. And in the winter, one eye seen through glass. A smile in eye—I could not mistake for mine. Now I don't know what to call you. Where you have gone. I consult the dictionary for advice. I find: a crucial point reached in a course of action with no possibility of turning back. A substance that can impair. A chemical action inside the body. Two opposite poles, as in a magnet. A purposely expressionless face. A sharp or tapering end. A mark of punctuation surrounded by large bright-red petallike leaves. To furnish a point, as in a pencil. Starting point — yourself: within water.

Love,
Gerda

You wrote the name *Gerda* for me. You watched my thought just as easily as Gerda watched Kai when he no longer existed. I had already become her. You knew that I would never submit to being a character who did not know her own tale. You knew that in trusting me to take up this role, each act of divination would be created anew and complete. You knew that in this way you'd made me responsible for locating yourself. For bringing you back from the land of winter. Never mind that we had already, in the outer worlds, drifted to Spring. You knew as you closed your eyes each night and did not sleep. I knew you had departed, like the artist who never arrived at the gallery. Like the blank sheet of snow. You left yourself and therefore me. How could I possibly blame you for separating? You had already separated from yourself.

River rejects shoe
Flowers deny earth

dear—

If there were a way to invoke messages without stopping, through fingertips. Fathom your reversals amid silt and ice. I can speak in sepals, from the underside of narrative. I'm not allowed to do this, but I go on because another time ago speaks a different language. Of what consequence is the word "unknown" or even "forbidden" to a dimensionless character, a string of letters? Of what consequence to retrace a speech of thumbs, buttons, breath beneath breath, fallen to the floor? Would you follow me, pick up each invisible utterance? Place the weightless pile delicately upon a chair? Would you stand and leave me there to unmend every space between known obstacles? Would you pull back the curtains and ask me to wait?

Dear Kai,

Now, look in the glass.

What if I were to carry this bundle of letters, breath beneath breath, weightless, those opposite to the ones published anonymously. Letters which have been erroneously attributed to others. What if I were to carry mine, and place them in that empty space, where once was a blank sheet of snow, in a gallery? Wood of a yew tree becomes bow. Wait on the will of broad, thick or course brushstrokes, a villainous character, a barrier or boundary. Heed— the state of a body perceived to generate sky—firmament.

Love,
Gerda

This is a tale of separation. Why is each human rent, hung, torn away from being-self-beloved? What are the marks we make upon our bodies to reveal or to disguise our frequent uncharitable journeys? If we travel we do so to keep our spirit company. This is what Gerda told herself. I sang it to myself mile by mile as I fell into each mathematical or conceptual project you supposed was just about reasons to meet in your flat at night. Excuses to undress and not sleep. We kept company with our mutual absence of sleep. Our mutual absence of personhood. Why had we abandoned ourselves? Is that the remedy of love? A remedy in verse is abstracted from bodies. You said you were weary of the idea of yourself. You wished to be tangential. An angle. A preposition. A character unmade. And so you permitted yourself. You climbed on the back of the frozen sleigh. You covered yourself in furs. You allowed yourself to be kissed.

I knew how to invent you even when you were the least probable of postulates. I never tired of unsolved bodies. I was weary of the wandering tale of separation. You promised me we would obliterate distances. You adorned me with capacious words. You placed them on my tongue. You wrote wide archives, orchards, at dusk, where we walked. We had an agreement that exertion must seamlessly relate to skin. We had an understanding which often did not involve words. More or less wading. Into each other. One, and yet absent.

Dear Kai,

Oh, what truly long dark winter days they were.

Where are you between snout and snub, formed from the freezing of water vapor in air. Shut in, immobilized, driven by wind, with drooping white flowers. A barrier, a figure resembling a human, a vehicle or machine adapted for clearing, a frame to prevent sinking, a storm you ignore. Trespasses and unwanted influences. A mirror which battles self. Curved horns of the elk. Do not pull down this veil into sedge or rushes. Your will is progress.

Love,
Gerda

dear—

Do you think I mind being only a string of pale letters? Do you know the acrostic written on a wire was not gendered? A poet wrote to me and said: Readers fear the woman inside a voice who spoke without sophistry, in sentences, and capes flung from borrowed, sleeping forms.

Your sight distorted—mirror shards in eye. With one kiss you have been numbed. Another locked lip stole your memory. But who loved you further and before? Before this story begins? In the tale I can only be a child who grows up one spring, but I've already told you—I'm finished being an abstraction. Famished.

Dear Kai,

He's not dead, said the roses.

My warm tears found—. One kiss removes numbness. A second restores memory. Tears unbind you. This syllabary contains no reverse.

An absent thrummed shadow, an incision in pavement, a heavy cloud synonym.

Woolen brow, circling, obfuscating.

I wished unbreakably that you might love me. And then you loved me.

Unknowable, ardent words—what am I without your inscrutable portents?

In the first divulged permutation of her tale I asked the sun. She asked swallows. Her "I" swam a murky legacy. No, "her" said, undoing her hem. That was not the first object of my tale, not the first telling. She unclasped the arms about her, and set them, his pale story arms, down upon a bench in the light. They looked like nothing. Not even snow. The story of the absent can be told in many ways. Ask the tulip tree but equally ask the trail of electronic communications, still open in your palm. Ask the invisible. Ask any stone you encounter on your way. Mother stone, sister stone. Ask your animal familiar. Ask the newspaper. Where has he gone? A pile of books atop your desk, open any at random, and ask.

Ask a river, with shoes

Kiss grandmother asleep

as ammunition

Then go and open

the gate   ask

Have you taken him, she asked the river, offering her blood-red shoes.

If the answer is yes, will you take me too?

No said the river

Which no, she asked

First no, spoke the river

And second is second, she said, each second beckons. Billows bother me, bully, stop butchering. The river laughed. Blustered—she took herself away.

I'm in love with you, the river conjured, conjoined. And the river followed her. But it was no use. She slipped back on her shoes and ran along the edges of murdered epithets. If you are taken away by ice you are escorted by heavily beaded condensation which clasps and begs, then ornaments your every breath, like a sphere of loaded mistresses, loaves of tread. If you are taken you are loaded like a presumptuous street bell, ovens of whereabouts, a vanquished tallow wing of ellipses.

His child-self told her that he knew how to do mental arithmetic, with fractions.

She told his absence to deduce, to describe the problem, in words and symbols upon the banks of clasps and loaded tallow presumptions.

She slipped back on her breath and loaded herself with trodden green shores.

Gerda asks herself: what to say to an absence? A blurred passage is born as she fails to wait. And yet simultaneously waits. By what name do you call the failure of waiting?

By what measure do we judge a failure of patience? Signs, rending of hands, speaking to ether, drowning the senses in darkness so as to better imagine arrival.

Days in which I've done nothing wrong are terrible. Days in which I tremble for my wrongdoing are worse. Days in which I imagine the impact of bodies, hear a crash in the distance, amid birdsong, are deftly packed and stowed for a later recurrence of light. Stretched out and questioned silently. Must we plead with our undone actions to lie fallow or come into being? And where is the prescribed text for such endeavors?

I saw a girl speaking to stones in this way. She laid them out along a ledge and spoke to them in turn: mother stone, bird stone, traveling stone, head stone. Then she danced, and made an arrangement of flowers. And then she asked the stones, quite solemnly, if they intended to come along.

III. The Book of Separating from One's Skin

\

I should not spend my time looking for a notebook lost. Though it is difficult to stop. My question to myself was what happens next in our letters? And what book am I writing? Whose ethereal pages?

How I miss writing since I came to life and left the page. I must begin to place myself within borders. Stop resisting every motion and meter of change.

I found you (as a character in a book).

Dear dream image

Reside, write
Inside only
Love one—book
framed by another
molting. Lost skin of
inside pages

Dear premise of fall
Dear not—dead not
Season leaden
colors laden, ripe

Dear trees fallen
Crested precipitation

Dear crown of red apples

What is dream?
Under mind, mowing

Crested colors, you

Dear dream image

A notebook lost will not stop waiting for a train. Looking, beginning, sitting on a bench in the Spring, the book of separating from one's own skin.

Fragile states—and who escorts. Rose—floating on air. Blotted precariousness—of thought body. After—follows. The book of sewing back on one's skin.

I found that once I had begun to believe a series of sentences I had spoken silently to myself, and written to you, I was unable to stop believing them. This mechanism of believing oneself to be in love is a state similar to looking for a notebook lost, a former self, once a body, now an idea, or a series of premonitions.

Yet I found that you—a character in a book still in the process of being written—had no objections to my writing sentences and attaching them to your lips. Dear extremely agreeable fictional companion: How could I blame myself for creating images composed in sky. Half awake. In your absence.

I wondered then, how I might translate all of the notebooks into the novel I was writing. The notebooks began with the problem that I would never be able to tell you. At first I found this frustrating. Hopeless even. Then I realized that writing the novel was an answer to the problem of falling in love with a character in a book who would not speak back. Like a rose floating in air. What does it mean?

In notebooks you might say whatever I wished. Still, I found I had to wait for your answers. I found I could write the silences as well as the distances. When you told me you loved me the book was temporarily ruined.

Each day I went out to greet the morning sky. To walk.

To greet roses which were synonymous

With floating compositions

How could I continue to write a book about an unarticulated love once that love had been written? I was so happy with our confessions that I was distracted from the problem in writing I had created.

Then I realized that my book was a fiction and what I needed was another story overlaid that was not ours.

Just as I chose a story from which to borrow, you wrote something to me in a letter, something that came from the story I had just stolen, and in that moment I realized that this series of mirrors would go on.

Where would our story depart from the stories we had borrowed to become ourselves? Where would page separate from person? Which stories were true and which fictions? Whose body of text had I written? Which blossoms detached from stem?

What is textual belonging? I knew that though we could not belong to each other in the physical world, in the realm of fiction anything was plausible. I took comfort in every myth or prevarication which I saw as linking us inextricably together, yet also leaving us distinct, intact, unattainable. We would never be possessed and in our independence we were free to imagine states which ignored separation. We were free not only to separate from our own skins but from our personal narratives.

A spell bound twin buds together, wrapped in ribbon.

I saw them decompose before and after, collapsed like a truth which cannot be told, only suspended.

I wanted to tell you about the books in which we were part human and part stone, part river spirits, part bird, part apparition. Part ocean, part humming.

In this new state not only did I have no shell, but I was reduced to innards, raw and laid upon the shore.

I asked how to have a shell. How to be a bivalve.

Disassociated landscapes danced before windows.

How to understand a landscape which isn't there? How to write the days as they decompose? Rush headlong into sleep.

How can one tell an innocent text from a blameless? Wrapped inside the blossom wing.

I wondered how you would taste detached from fictional names

In real life, if life within a body were real, then we would have no such freedom

So why wish to be anything beyond lettered?

How to translate—?

The last thing written in the lost notebook is "inside infinite tenderness"

Would anyone see, under barely wakening skies

I went outside at dawn to inhale—the rooms inside the rose

(I will transcribe and translate another notebook, remaking the experience of one fictional character—who also writes in a journal. Or is it the opposite, taking notes from life and transposing them to fiction? The difference becomes difficult to divide. Person from page. Fiction from form. Narrative from language. As if there were only one set of arrows).

Words written on a rose still slightly fragrant. I have no time to assemble myself. I cannot ask the runes or the cards. My question is no longer a question but a series of strewn petals, pages. I should learn another language. A non-figurative language.

Where begins the book of separation from one's life?

I like to leave the first page blank

When your letter arrives will I recognize your handwriting?

Or will it be a senseless script which penetrates one with strangeness of stepping out onto an unknown precipice?

Separated from my own skin by several meters or by fracture of seasons

I could write constantly but question the impulse

Why does love desire to describe oneself as if one has never existed before?

I hope that writing in public places will rearrange me

The answer is always to write

Either we are only words and words are free and innocent or words create the worlds

Bliss is also constraint. That your words may bring joy and your silence distress. How can this be when I cannot even conjure an image of your face or the sound of your voice? How can this be when walking down a crowded street I don't even know if I would recognize you?

IV. An Endless Chain of Persons Who Are Not You

In a gallery, a four-foot by four-foot square slab of ice, opaque white, inset several feet below the floor. Around the slab is a question, cordoning off the area. How difficult could it be to solve for authorship? A plaque on the wall upon entering the small room reads "Letters Inscribed in Snow." Our eyes are blank, bare. The artist who used a pseudonym becomes a nondeterministic solution. The number of agents who installed the question—obscured by departure. Failure to identify the artist cracks the ice of an unwritten book. Surely the real author or the real artist would burn blue lights in the evening.

In the dream which remains unwritten and unchaste, the dream which is never dreamed but only imagined, we occupied actual bodies in space and we were one. In the dream overlying that dream, in which the everyday becomes a prayer and a series of actions prone to the limits of gravity and rotations of planets—in that dream we became real. But that dream could never be written, only lived. If we were to live that dream then we would become breathing persons. To look into each other's eyes once, or a handful of times, to place my hands on your shoulders, could last a long time. But there is always a point at which to live with another, on a daily basis, involves a transfer of attentions, a transfer of the real to the unreal, and back again.

dear—

I want to be writing my new novel. But I have not begun. I've
hidden my gardens underground. My thoughts are sewing threads.
When the right theoretical question (which I plan to steal) falls in
front of me , I will begin.

And one of the central dialects will be:
Are the icicles asleep or are they dead?

And another will be, what is a letter?

What does the snowdrop inscribe?

Or maybe the book is made up entirely of archaic crystals found
on the pavement

Or about to be performed by a vanished ice sheet

Or fictional accounts of kissing roses

Or a dying planet drawn as a forest thicket—across a city diadem

The everyday is ecstatic and prone to limitations. If I lived within actions, or woke beyond a screen of backlit words, maybe then I could stop this ridiculous idealization. But until that time which may not exist, I cling to notions which outshine the imperfect. I remain within the written, where I may touch without limit, retreat from a world which wants to decide, which moves incrementally in one direction through time, a world in which the unsolvable is ignored. Instead I walk above treelines. All constraints have been removed and we speak in phrases culled from letters.

Sitting in a café, I put down the few words on a rose I had been reading. They were published under your name but I was doubtful. You have many names and this was one encoded by a regiment of snowflakes. The snowflakes ran along the ground and the nearer they came the larger they grew.

Divinity wrote me a letter. At first I feared you might lapse, as I do in private, into fears which cannot be addressed, or that you would disappear entirely. But you always return to the page, adhere. You wrote to me once, long before the way in which we converse now, something begun in winter, which startled me awake. I began to cry. I could not catch my breath. I wanted to disbelieve your words. Did you mean what you said? Unsteady as I write, drafting a new loneliness which did not exist before. Your sky is gold, flaxen, spreading.

I was supposed to meet you at the café. I put the few words on a rose back into my bag and tried to concentrate, my head bent over fields and piles of blue evenings. I kept looking up to the plate glass window, laced with white crystals, each time the door opened. In came many persons. Breath poured out of their mouths like smoke. But each time I looked up it was not you who entered and after a while I lost track of how long I had been waiting. What an endless chain of persons who are not you. Suddenly when you did appear I closed my eyes for a moment because I disbelieved what I saw. Where have you been all this time? And where have I been? As we went through the door together arm in arm I noticed we had both become children.

Is it possible to say everything and confess nothing? Yes, but that is also a form of prevarication. I could wait to write until I have gained a false mastery of my emotions—but what would that reveal? As I pause pink trees behind me on the screen tremble. In the most intimate of acts I ask myself this question: Is the book of separating from one's life synonymous with impossible love? How dangerously we allow the days to flee.

Later you sent me a message I did not entirely understand. I had wished for a spectacular meeting and instead I wondered if I had been speaking to a snow labyrinth. The message relayed an unsolved maze, which you noted as the most notorious problem of winter gardens—gone underground. You summarized the problem like this: "And when they were tired and lay down, they arranged themselves in the very letters." You mentioned that the problem would be difficult to take by the hand, but practical applications included a pair of new skates. If the solution to a problem can be verified in shining pieces of ice, can it be inscribed in polynomial-winds abated by sun-time? In order to find a solution, one must first locate a book of exponential hands. But your movements disorient my meaning. What is your meaning? You try to overcome the difficulty of unsolved isolation by breaking down the separation between the body of any given season and the more than one-hundred ice halls, according to the way the winds shift. You tell me this is how you define breath.

Addressed in tones of love. With each day that this does not happen I am distressed. I am to blame. I am caught in useless thoughts. What is the point in separating from one's life in this manner? The energy that it requires of me to reframe things in a positive light is equal to freezing. I find it appalling that no one can read my thoughts.

V. Instantaneous Book of Silence

Three dreams of you, in which you do not appear. The first is ice and bridges, possibly my own death, a reckless search at night. The second dream has been stolen from my memory. In the third dream you are sitting across from me, in a meadow, in Spring. I am deliriously happy thinking I may finally see you. And yet you do not appear. The sun is shining in my eyes, upon your image, so brightly, you are obliterated by light.

In relating a narrative in a straightforward manner something is buried. Undergarment or undertale. An approaching archive of untamed prose.

You read seamlessly at the edge of a river, amid the rush of novelistic water.

You pause to say, please don't call me Hallimede, or Metis.

I answer, please don't call me Sedna or Gerda.

When I ask about the letters we wrote and placed in the gallery, you pause from your calculations and look up at me. You are so tired, you say, of all of the misrepresentations and false letters. Even ours.

Obviously, we made everything up.

No, you answer, we wrote one chain. And the others?

You look at me as if I could possibly know. We are in your studio. All around us are piles of pages, letters you have sent to me, poems created by chance. You look at me as if some unknown alphabet has been thrust between us.

I must have known that you were not asking if I had written any of the other letters. In this moment of non-speech between us I saw clearly that I was being accused, but of what I was being accused I had no idea. A book of silence instantaneously arose. Did your gaze communicate animosity that you did not know what you should certainly know? Either you were the "I" to whom I was now speaking, or we were someone else, a small circle of pseudonyms we had become. Probably, we both imagined we were with someone else who had been standing around that night at the gallery, looking at the blank slab of snow. This was the real reason why the publication of the letters, their circulation, had caused so much distress. The letters were an endless source of speculation.

There we were at all hours, groping, working on this question of completeness, nakedness, on conditions, positions which might satisfy a question. We had become the question in episodic wanderings. We knew nothing about the coldness of time, but we became a series of correspondences, architectures of modernist desire.

How fractional at times is our speech, white, opaque, eroding. How much do you know about the ground on which you stand? You ask me this question out of doors, at night. You put down the letter in your hand. I've never asked you which name is yours, which are false adornments. I've never asked why you insist upon so many names. I don't know when all names, all symbols, all signs between us became fictions. How fractional are your arms? How fractional is your sight?

dear—

I've lost my way within the book I am writing, and yet writing is the only way ahead. Elation gave way to devastation and I have barely begun. Though I've entered many times, beginning with this paragraph, inscribed in snow. I remember only a written thicket above and below the hidden.

If my thoughts are unfathomed, if you remain an unwritten fiction, how can I possibly steal you?

How I love your dream / poem / letter. I realize now that what I wrote to you last was not at all adequate to what I wish to say. How grateful I am to read your words. To read you. To read the space between our letters. What I wish is to offer you as much pleasure as you can endure. How much can a dying fiction endure? How can dying be an impetus for correspondence?

The book begins where touch and taste become apparitions.

The book begins where you invariably vanish— become real.

dear—

Transmutation. Doubly bound. Lips may not speak and hands may not write. Lips may not kiss and hands may not touch.

When awake I imagine a dream which does not arrive. In the dream we wake and ask if we are dreaming. Or we arrive at night, to meet and ask the same question. Yes, we are both dreaming. Yes, the dream is real. Is this happening in a letter or is it actual? Writing is actual. What constitutes consummation? What obliges me to say to myself, or to you, anything?

From the place of the nameless I look out a window. The snow, thick and unplowed, appears as a soft white mantle. In this paragraph which character speaks? Someone has turned, been bewitched. Who? Should I reveal this in the text or keep it hidden? Or maybe I should use this compositional voice as well, to debate what should be revealed. The truth is I don't know, so how could I possibly reveal anything? What constitutes betrayal? What constitutes faithfulness?

I look out the window again and ask myself what I have ruined by such an admission. Why look out, away from interiors? I am married to a text in which an excellent love plagues me. My own silence falls upon the page. Would it be any different if one of the characters were actual? Might it be easier if real letters arrived from real persons? Would it be different if one could translate this notion of a drowning love, the moment of falling in love, into something continuous: a chain of letters. Would I just go on with my life gladly as if nothing were happening, or would the imaginary object of love become so woven into my thoughts that I would not recognize when you appear? Might I breathe an audible sigh of relief to find myself not thinking of you? The mind knows impossibility yet pursues. But what does it pursue?

You thought mathematics would assuage such questions, equations, and therefore you determined and convinced me to try severe hypotheses, involving real persons, strangers as well as intimates. You handed me a narrative and asked me to go out and rehearse love. You told me not to come back until I could answer for our characters. Is it possible to be satisfied in a relationship constructed solely of text? In a world in which blankness, snow, page, obliterates any nature of the landscape? In which the characters beneath become: netting, tulle, icon, lace? Go and find them, you begged.

dear—

In the dream you are on my right. I only know this because I can hear your voice. You are telling me, at night, without words, how to illuminate anything in the world, as a method of writing. Gold parentheses are cast, encircling an image. Your arms reach up, into indigo. And find. A tiny bird. A halo.

I want to see your face but I know, if I open my eyes, you will vanish. Like the dream about to be written, the bird you inscribe exists delicately. Such carefulness is required in approach so as not to startle a non-corporeal image held in mind. We are in spirit partially erased—existing within limits of a physical world. Somewhere distant the eyes set in our sleeping bodies appear closed.

Dear Gerda,

When I first arrived at the ice palace, my brain and body adapted to the pitching and tilting that naturally occurs. Around one notion of a planetary system is another which continually enlarges perception. As we stood examining the absent letters in snow you began to speak about a recent discovery. Snow blind. For the first time in my life I have been somewhere. Increased tears and a feeling of pain, likened to having sand in the eyes. Scientists have spotted a new dwarf planet at the edge of our solar system. Arc eye. Welder's flash. Flash burns. Discomfort at bright light. Less commonly searing sea or sand. Pink ice far beyond Pluto. Blackening the skin underneath the eyes with charcoal. Astronomers used to believe that there was nothing in this area. Blackening the seas beneath eyes. Isolation in a dark room. Until recently, the only object detected in that part of our solar system was a dwarf planet called Sedna, named after an Inuit goddess said to live in the Arctic Ocean. For the first time I wonder which hand is mine. When we left the gallery you continued to talk about sight, about planetary systems, about ice as preserver.

We were still looking down to the ground covered in ice. Writing under the influence of an extreme spell. Which forward? Which ahead? A motion or bobbing sensation that tends to disappear when moving and reappear when still. I was curious about the artist. Shall we call her Sedna, you asked? Smiling you reached for my hand, but when I searched your face your expression was a moment later, blank, bare. For the first time in my life I have dispelled the inner roving. Trying to walk on a mattress or trampoline. I had wanted to discuss the identity of the missing artist, or the unwritten story. But you continued to tell me that the difficulty in sighting more objects in this region is that such distant things don't emit their own light. For the first time I have released the oars, succumbed. The Inuit carved snow goggles from caribou antlers to help prevent snow blindness. Curved to fit the face. A long thin slit cut to allow in a small amount of light. Held to the head by a cord made of caribou sinew. I walked ahead blinded. Light from the sun has to travel billions of miles out, reflect off the object, then travel billions of miles back. Along the way some light is lost. A background understanding of my condition may help to hasten my voyage and prevent my disappearance after a sleigh voyage is complete.

Imagine, you say to me, that we are standing on this newly discovered planet. So rare, this sense of prolonged dizziness or imbalance is all I ever wanted. The real artist is disembarking. You asked me who wrote the letters? So new, not yet given names. If we were standing on this ball of ice it would be cold, pink. Letters drenching my hands as they melt. Laden, collapse. A sleigh, melting. Minus four hundred degrees Fahrenheit. Dark. Our sun would appear only as an ordinary, distant star.

Love,
Kai

Dear Gerda,

I told myself that this tomb of ice must have been a gallery. That I looked not into a tomb but a trove of letters. I told myself we resided on various planets, with a myriad of names, and mathematics could remove me from winter. I know I must go further. When I look at the horizon all movement stops. Whose retina, on a boat? Bats overhead consent. Who describes who? No one uses this perambulating library of sleet, flurry, blizzard, drift. Birds laugh along the seashore, though I must be imagining sand as ice. Though my hands would surely shake. Dear Gerda, I have written these crystallized letters on ledgers of ice and I pray that they may reach you. Here, from within my head. If I write your name repeatedly will you appear? Your name means: Twig, spear, protector, guarded. Gerd. Enclosure. Wife of Freyr.

Love,
Kai

Dear Gerda,

Who is Freyr? And why should he deserve you? I am told I am keeper of keys, earth, unbreakable. I am triumphant, pier, probably water. My name means also restoration, recovery, willow tree. Have any of these names helped me? Not in the least. I'm told I once had a friend named Gerda, as all surfaces pitch and tilt. I am told I will soon be released. What will it be like to emerge? Liquid sunlight? Is your garden still underground? I write to you from the Bethelm Royal Hospital, from below stairs a parlor, a kitchen, two larders, a long entry throughout the house, and 21 rooms wherein poor distracted people lie. I write to you from the trade in literacy. I write to you from a madhouse of the seventeenth century. I write to you from humanitarian reform. From behind several sheets of dark paper, behind which I hide. I am here under pretense of research. Please forgive my long silence. The truth is I don't know where to send this letter. I don't know if you exist at all, or if I invent you in order to invent this tale.

Love,
Kai

Dear Gerda,

The truth is that one will never know what another thinks. I enter into writing like trying to cram myself into a car, wedged in without adequate space. I torque neck and back in ways you would find not at all practical in your dress or tall boots, in my frock coat of rain. I insert myself, as if I were a book, crammed in between other books, a phantom, as if my spine could be placed there, shelved. Yet if I were a book I would not attempt to document this process.

Trying to get into the head of "she" when "she" is so elusive is like light which will not illuminate. "She" turns her head as you approach so "you" cannot see her face. "She" evades "you." You know that you will know nothing until meeting. You have been waiting. And this voice speaking now must also be her voice. Until you reach the final voice in a series of voices which might be your own.

(This last paragraph is the final "she" discussing herself in the novel inscribed in snow. "She" of disappearances is part elegy, part dream, part summoning. But that is also a lie. This last paragraph has finally arrived, and one sees that "she," the final she, whatever her name, has no more access to her own thoughts than any previous speaker).

To exit one's window and walk to the train is to see many bodies. Stimulus does not dissipate. I keep beginning, looking at what it is to be human, with café sounds. Finally you arrive. We've rarely existed and the barista looks at us critically with one non-fictional eye.

September is forever again. Borrowed. I wish to clear my desk, my other body—a plea.

Attraction—to disappear entirely from one's life. What does it mean? Maybe, if I were brave, that would be the novel I would write, about the man who spends a large portion of his day fantasizing and so the reader might believe this is true but in the end it is not a book he is writing. No one is betrayed (or maybe it is also the book he is writing). Understory—add integrated arcs on disappearing and call this: a disappearing text. Start with the perspectives of others (collective imagination). I need to find out my name. In this text Kai disappears and Gerda tries to locate him, but that narrative is just a stand-in for every character one becomes, and the person who is lost to oneself. Interchangeable subjects subject themselves to whatever they say.

Or maybe she, the character "she" as she will be named "she" compared to all other she's in the text, is now the next installment. Does she will the book to come apart?

The "he" disappearing does so about a person who does not exist. Person is always book. Book is always body. Body is always found.

There are writers who want to write about the world disappearing and there are writers who want to live as if personhood were intact.

Approach personhood now. Later does not exist.

I walk willingly away from many who could help me. I am alarmed at the things my fingers wish to say.

I am waiting until the text permits my entrance. Text like a dress which you cannot reach to zip in the back, click little hook into eye. Snagged, one's feet hurt, and the dancers on stage stop to brush stray hair out of their eyes, to adjust their undergarments in full view as part of the performance. Note to hands, stop checking. There is nothing you need to know, known, knows. Who knows what this is all about? Who will come home with rigging? Who despite a skeleton could call you into question about inner scaffolding? Your inner scaffolding, ask yourself, is it a web of well taut lies, fragile? Think filaments the color of air, a wonder it can support anything. And when the leaves are turning color above you, and when you are watching them arc, turn and fall, what is turning inside that I fail to register, that I fail to lament, that I refuse to see, right in front of me? That is the subject of my mourning, or my celebration, or book.

Love,
Kai

dear—

1. You, first person, in every switchback, are riveting. The speaker is every character. Though we are never sure when. Each narration is a letter being written to one, picked up and written over by another.

2. Insatiably writing letters, as a fix, compulsively: recipients unable to answer.

3. Begin with an inscription, an address, at the top of an unlined page: a letter, which becomes a novel.

4. Observe and record strange inward habits of writers. Solitude broken by research requiring others entering—in texts—prevarications.

5. Employ confusion of identity, as an object, in fiction.

6. Glitter of surface tension betrays. We wish to be authentically stranded.

7. Address the problem of belief. Is any beloved actual? Writing as disguise. Veil of fingers. Eclipse of alphabets.

8. Can one walk, speak, breathe amid only a gravity of letters?

9. The problems of narration are the same insidious persons, containing prose, spores, potions, poses—open.

Dear Gerda,

I was in love or I wished that I were in love. Or I had written that I was. Inside a letter. I thought by telling no one, repeatedly, yet residing inside the written, it would become actual.

Yet these are merely sentences broken, distorted and remaindered. My words— by virtue of being disarranged—are my only vehicles. A frozen sleigh inscribed in sheets of ice. Leaf skeletons melting. Alphabets of eyes describe an inscrutable silence. Collapse in the hands of their makers.

I wrote a sentence or I thought that I had written a sentence. I moved my hand along the page and waited. I thought that a sentence could love. I was in love with a particular sentence. Who had written it? Did I imagine that the coldness surrounding me was also made of language? If I wrote different words would I be revealed?

I was a letter. Or I wished to reside in lines. A sentence sought to be made. Only inside a written love could I become real.

Love,
Kai

We are standing, embedded in epistolary histories, sunken and opaque. Around our letters are notations, envelopes, and boxes, officially cordoning off the words we have written. The cover of the box is marked by pseudonyms. We did not show up, failed to answer questions. We clearly intended an unwritten and therefore open book. What is the meaning of authorship—when one refuses to wake? We stand on frozen ground trying to divine what is beneath. Upon which inscription do we stand?

And now I want to write another letter, a letter so brief, a breath, to say I wish to be written by your pen. I want to be translated from a person into letters, to exist as pure language, to travel that way, with the complete liberty of a letter, to reside inside your eye, your mouth, your hand. Transcribe me, please, until I may travel easily through the ether.

I dreamed again of the bird

you illuminate in a dream

into the frame or blank page

a field of snow

absent of color

bird about to be written

dear—

We did not rewrite our names. For this reason you spoke to me
only in eyes, and motions by which no one else could approach.
When we arrived at the unspeakable there was nothing more.
We laughed into the quiet placed about our necks. We removed
embellishments. Breath became speech where fields of ice blindness
were given up in favor of bedding. Synonyms adorned our eyes.
We met in the place where alphabets had been abandoned, and
roses, now unread, could exist above or below ground.

dear—

Lovers of letters impaled by time and circumstance. To exist beyond the page one is required to keep writing, and then to lift the page to one's eyes. To take it in hand.

You put down the book and looked up. A consensual meeting of eyes in the first person, on the penultimate page, would not disappoint premises hidden between covers. Still we wondered how to vacate the confines of fiction and write ourselves into beginning.

Acknowledgements:

Versions of this text originally appeared in the following journals: *Conjunctions*, *Golden Handcuffs Review*, *Journal of Poetics Research*, and *Tinderbox*. Thank you Bradford Morrow, Lou Rowan, Molly Sutton Kiefer and John Tranter for your generous support of this work.

Excerpts from this book originally appeared as a chaplet titled *Amulets and Letters*, published by Belladonna. Thank you to Krystal Languell, Rachel Levitsky, and the Belladonna Collective.

Thank you Marcella Durand, Airea Dee Matthews for readings and encouragement. Thank you to everyone at Tinderbox for your dedication and support of this work, especially Molly Sutton Kiefer and Nikkita Cohoon. Many thanks to Erica Baum for her artwork.

Grateful acknowledgement to the Pew Foundation for a fellowship and a MacDowell Colony residency, which supported the writing of this book.

Laynie Browne's recent publications include: a book of poems, *Translation of the Lilies Back into Lists*, a novel, *Periodic Companions*, and a book of short fiction, *The Book of Moments*. Her work has appeared in journals such as *Conjunctions*, *A Public Space*, *New American Writing*, *The Brooklyn Rail*, and in anthologies including: *The Ecopoetry Anthology*, *The Reality Street Book of Sonnets*, and *Postmodern American Poetry:A Norton Anthology*. Her poetry has been translated into French, Spanish, Chinese and Catalan. She co-edited the anthology *I'll Drown My Book: Conceptual Writing by Women* and edited the anthology *A Forest on Many Stems: Essays on The Poet's Novel*. Honors and awards include a Pew Fellowship, the National Poetry Series Award for her collection *The Scented Fox*, and the Contemporary Poetry Series Award for her collection *Drawing of a Swan Before Memory*. She teaches at University of Pennsylvania.